Presented to:

_____

From:

_____

Date:

_____

I've Just Seen Jesus

SANDI PATTY & LARNELLE HARRIS

J. Countryman
Nashville, Tennessee

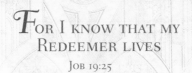

For I know that my
Redeemer lives

Job 19:25

A Note from Sandi

If there is one thing that I have learned in my lifetime, it is this—*There is absolutely nothing that compares to a personal encounter with Jesus, the Christ.*

Larnelle Harris and I have been singing this song for over fifteen years, and it is interesting to me that the inspirational impact never seems to diminish. It is even more sobering to realize that the song's message is more powerful to me now than at any point in my lifetime. Although I personally committed my life to Jesus when I was eight years old, there have been many times since then that I have had to reacquaint myself with Him.

I've sung about God's love, forgiveness, and grace for so many years, and I have always believed them to be true. However, there was a season of my life, several years ago, when I was making wrong and sinful choices. Through much prayer, conviction, and loving and truthful confrontation by godly

people, I realized I had strayed far away from what I knew to be true and right. One very cold, stormy night, stranded at an airport at my wit's end, on the phone with my pastor, I had a personal encounter with Jesus.

I remember so clearly the feeling of finally letting go, of saying, "No matter what, I want to be right and clean before you, Lord." When I got up off that airport floor, I could already sense the change taking hold in my heart. I had seen, felt, and embraced Jesus in the most personal way, and I knew I would never be the same.

My favorite lyric in this song says,
And I knew, He really saw me, too
It was as if 'til now
I'd never lived

All that I'd done before
Won't matter anymore
God is an awesome God, and His grace is still so amazing!

Sandi Patty

A Note from Larnelle

I've often wondered what those present at the crucifixion were thinking as they witnessed our Savior on the cross. I've come to realize that much of modern day thought and action can be traced to those present at this event.

A reading of the Scriptures reveals some pretty familiar faces in attendance. First to come to mind are the disciples, the chosen—those privileged with almost constant fellowship with the Master. But when it was certain that Jesus would be crucified, their response was probably predictable. They, like many today, did not fully understand who He was, and when the going got tough, they got going! Essentially, they were no longer willing to risk their lives to be identified with Him.

Who else was there? The religious. Even in the presence of deity, this crowd lacked the spiritual insight to recognize the Christ. Their strong commitment to ritual caused them to see Jesus as another radical with influence. Because His views threatened the status quo, He needed to be removed. They perceived themselves as protectors of present and future generations and thought they needed to cast out the ideals and principles of the "opiate of the people."

And we can't forget the Romans. There are always those who just do not seem to care which way the voting goes. Though choosing to abstain is sometimes a good strategy, failing to have an opinion seems to me as disastrous as not being given the right to participate in decisions that affect you directly. But the Romans simply wanted to wash their hands of the whole business. After all, it didn't effect them! How wrong they were.

Against such a backdrop of witnesses, it becomes clear why, today, in the midst of an "I'm-okay, you're-okay worldview," the message of a risen, living Savior keeps coming back in word, deed, and—yes—music. How thankful I am for that handful of personage at Golgotha who did not fully

comprehend it all, yet still believed.

The world continually parrots its views, hoping that something heard often enough will eventually be regarded as true. In the face of such confusing messages, however, believers must never tire of bearing witness to the existence of a merciful, forgiving, miracle-working, *living Lord* whose every spoken word and deed bare repeating.

I've just seen Jesus. I tell you He's alive.

Larnelle Harris

Susanne's Story

I checked my husband into the hospital one morning at 6:30 for a right rotator-cuff repair. We knew he was in good hands because this doctor had successfully operated on Henry's left shoulder, with no problems.

His operation started; it would take about ninety minutes. I was in Henry's room at 9 a.m. when the operating room nurse called. She said all was going well, and it would be another thirty to forty-five minutes. That was good news. Henry would be in the hospital only one day.

I was hanging his clothes in the closet when Dr. Thomas, who is also our family friend, walked in at 9:15; he had a strange look on his face. I was surprised to see him and said, "Well, that was quick!" Then he hugged me and started to cry. He told me that Henry's heart had stopped.

Dr. Thomas said, "Susanne, I don't know what happened . . . but Henry's heart stopped on the operating table. We are working on him, but it doesn't look good. We need to pray."

The doctors, nurses, and technicians did all they had been trained to do to save a life, but *after ninety minutes of a flat line on the monitor*, the cardiologist called "the code." *Henry had not survived.* The operating room staff put away the paddles. Dr. Thomas looked at the body and wondered how he was going to tell me that Henry had died.

Dr. Nirste, the cardiologist, looked over at Dr. Thomas and said, "Paul, we did all that we could do."

Our church friends had filled two rooms as they prayed, and I had been praying a selfish prayer, asking God to touch Henry's heart and let him live

because we had been married just four years. I wanted him with me, although I knew that heaven would be blessed to have him.

In the operating room, everything is counted in minutes and seconds. About five seconds after Dr. Nirste made his statement and after ninety minutes of flat line, the heart monitor suddenly went *beep . . . beep . . . beep.*

The Great Physician had come into the room and touched Henry!

There is no physical damage. There is no mental damage. There is no emotional damage. There is only joy and wonder!

To God be the glory!

Susanne Ray

Henry's Story

When I went into the hospital for routine shoulder surgery on September 4, 1998, I woke up expecting my shoulder to be hurting, but instead, my chest was killing me. I had an oxygen mask on my face and a tube down my throat, and my hands were tied down. This was not what I remembered from my first shoulder operation!

I knew people from my church had been there praying for me, but when I heard one of my pastors saying, "Henry, you better not scare us like that again!" I had no idea why he said that. Then I heard Dr. Thomas talking to my wife, Susanne, telling her that even though "he" was back, there might be paralysis, brain damage, or kidney failure. I wondered if they were talking about me, and if they were, where had I been?

I looked down at my feet, which were sticking out from under the sheet, and

CALL TO ME, AND I WILL ANSWER YOU.
JEREMIAH 33:3

thought if I could just move my toes, then they must not be talking about me. So, I tried, and my toes moved, but no one saw them. Then I thought I would try to raise my feet and legs. I could do that also, but no one saw that either. I then assumed that they were not talking about me because I could move my toes and my feet.

In a little while, my wife came to my bedside. She said she had something important to tell me. She then told me that I had died in the operating room and was dead for an hour and a half, but after ninety minutes, God had started my heart back again. When she said those words, I began to cry. I wondered why in the world God would have chosen someone like me to be a part of a miracle like this since there was so much sin in my life. I still don't have that answer.

People from all over the hospital heard the news. They came to my room to look at me, to touch me, or to say a few words to me. One nurse called me "the miracle man," but I never knew what happened and don't remember a thing.

I didn't see heaven or hell or angels or a light at the end of a tunnel. I just felt as if I was under God's protection the entire time. Dr. Thomas said he had felt compelled to keep working on me, even though there were no signs of activity on the heart monitor. My heart was shocked sixteen times, and CPR was continuous. But a few seconds after all human lifesaving efforts had ceased, the monitor started beeping again.

My doctor said there was no medical reason for my heart to stop or for it to start again. He just knew that after the staff had stepped aside, the Greater Physician took over.

A week or so later, I was rechecked,

and the doctors found that even after that length of time with incomplete oxygen to my brain, I had no brain damage, no kidney problems, no paralysis, and no damage, scarring, or bruising to my heart. In fact, the doctors say I have a "perfect heart."

When Dr. Thomas was asked what finally worked for me on that very special day, he said, "Nothing I did worked. Medically, we could not get Henry back. It was the healing power of God. When we stopped, God took over. I witnessed a miracle that day . . . we all did."

Henry Ray

MUSHROOMS FROM HEAVEN

The Pacific Beer Garden in Chicago was for sale. Long regarded as the most notorious and murderous bar in the Midwest, it was filled nightly with alcohol, drugs, gambling, and the darkest figures of the underworld.

Imagine, then, how surprised Chicagoans were when they awoke one morning in 1880 and read that a sweet Christian couple, George and Sarah

Clarke, had purchased the lease for the Pacific Beer Garden.

Promptly dropping the word *Beer*, the couple added the word *Mission*, and launched a ministry to homeless alcoholics and downtrodden men and women. Thus was born the now world-famous ministry of the Pacific Garden Mission of Chicago—the Old Lighthouse—the second oldest rescue mission in the United States.

In the early years, Colonel and Mrs. Clarke bore the cost of the mission themselves, but as expenses grew and the ministry expanded, their funds ran low. Eventually the day came when they could not pay the rent. Attempts to secure funds failed, and Colonel Clarke was told that he had only twenty-four hours to make the payment or the Mission would close.

Throughout the night, Colonel and Mrs. Clarke prayed, asking God to guide and to provide in His own way and time. They reminded the Lord of the souls being saved each night, of the men and women whose lives were being salvaged. They asked Him why they should find

themselves in such straits while trying to do His work. But, determining to trust and not question, they remained before the throne of grace in simple faith and in earnest pleading until dawn.

When they emerged from their house that morning, they gasped. What had happened to their front yard? It was covered with something white, something that instantly reminded them of the manna of the Old Testament. Looking closer, they discovered their lawn was filled with mushrooms of the very best quality, which was quite mysterious because it wasn't the season for mushrooms.

Gathering the crop, the Clarkes carted the mushrooms down the street and sold them to the chefs at the Palmer House, the famed hotel just off of Michigan Avenue, for a large price. The receipts were enough to pay the rent, with enough left over to meet other ministry expenses.

Years later, "Mother" Clarke commented on the experience. "No mushrooms were ever seen there before—nor any since," she said.

MOTHER CLARKE AND JIMMY THE RAT

After the death of her husband, Sarah Clarke continued the work of the Pacific Garden Mission, her heart beating with endless love for down-and-outers. One of her favorites was Jimmy the Rat.

While growing up on a farm south of Chicago, Jimmy had become addicted to drugs. By age twenty, he was inhabiting the sewers of Chicago, doped and hopeless. His home became an opium den disguised as a laundry. There Jimmy pumped himself full of opium, morphine, and cocaine and slept away his life in a long, dark basement with boarded, street-level windows. Along the walls were double tiers of bunks where, from time to time, the white, pale faces of addicts would stare blankly from pillows.

One Sunday afternoon, lying in a stupefied slumber, Jimmy heard the sound of voices wafting through the boarded windows. From a nearby bunk, someone mumbled, "Listen to the Pacific Garden Mission boys singing down the street." Jimmy slid from his bunk and staggered up to the door, listening to the words of the old hymn: *I am so glad that Jesus loves me; Jesus loves even me . . .*

Suddenly a hand jerked Jimmy back into the room and threw him roughly on the concrete floor. Later, he was carried from the house more dead than alive and thrown in the trash pile of a construction site, left to die in the driving rain.

Jimmy could never remember afterward how he got to the Mission that

> ONE GLIMPSE OF THE KING AND YOU ARE CONSUMED BY A DESIRE TO SEE MORE OF HIM AND SAY MORE ABOUT HIM.
> MAX LUCADO

night, but he staggered in during an evangelistic service.

Throwing up both hands, he cried, "I want somebody to pray for me!"

Mother Clarke quickly stepped from the platform, put her hand on his arm, and led him to a front seat. There she knelt by his pew, and he fell to his knees by her side. Mission workers gathered, and prayers were offered . . . and Jimmy the Rat met Jesus the Savior.

Jimmy's life was permanently transformed. Returning to the plains of Indiana, he became an outspoken Christian, a successful farmer, and in time, a godly husband and father who seized every opportunity to declare that no one is beyond the reach of the grace of the Lord Jesus Christ.

It was His voice she first heard
Those kind gentle words
Asking what was her reason for tears
And I sobbed in despair
"My Lord is not there"
He said, "Child! It is I! I am here!"

I've just seen Jesus
I tell you He's alive
I've just seen Jesus
Our precious Lord alive
And I knew, He really saw me too
As if 'til now I'd never lived
All that I'd done before
Won't matter anymore

I've just seen Jesus

I've just seen Jesus

I've just seen Jesus

And all I've ever done before

Won't matter anymore

I've just seen Jesus

And I'll never be the same again

I've just seen Jesus

THE CROSS OF CHRIST

One of Christianity's best-known leaders—recognized around the world—vanished in 1929. No clue as to his fate has ever emerged.

His name was Sundar Singh, and he was born into a wealthy family in India in 1889. His mother trained him from birth to become a Sikh holy man, and by age seven, he could quote by heart vast portions of Hindu holy books. Seeing his intelligence, his mother eventually sent him to a Presbyterian school for a one-year course in English. There Sundar was forced to read the New Testament, but he rebelled, raging against his missionary teachers. Being tall, good-looking, and muscular, he quickly became the leader of the anti-Christian students, on one occasion burning a Bible, page by page, before them.

But Sundar's white-hot emotions couldn't absorb the death of his mother, and he found himself at age fifteen overcome with despair. On Sunday night, December 17, 1904, he went to bed planning to commit suicide before breakfast. He rose according to plan at 3 a.m., took a ceremonial cold bath in keeping with Hindu custom, and prepared to cast himself in front of the 5 a.m. express train speeding by his house.

But as Sundar prayed, a light suddenly illumed the room, shining so brightly that he thought the house ablaze. A strong, serene figure seemed to appear in a vaporous white cloud and in perfect Hindustani spoke these words: "Why do you persecute me? Remember that I gave my life for you upon the cross."

Sundar, instantly converted to Christ,

felt enraptured in billows of joy and peace. When he later shared the news with his family, they were appalled, and failing to dissuade him, they tried to poison him. But Sundar, not to be denied, was baptized on his sixteenth birthday. He sought theological training and soon put on the yellow robe and turban of a sadhu, a wandering holy man, to go forth preaching the Gospel.

Through the mountain passes and over the rugged hills of northern India he journeyed, braving hardship and persecution. He was imprisoned. He was stoned. He was stripped and tortured with leeches. He was thrown into wells, naked, to die. His travels were so rigorous that he was called the "Apostle of the Bleeding Feet."

> "WHY DO YOU SEEK THE LIVING AMONG THE DEAD? HE IS NOT HERE, BUT IS RISEN!"
> LUKE 24:5–6

Yet his dark, shining eyes, full beard, and graceful poise reminded people of the Savior, and many believed he looked expressly like Jesus. His fame spread, and he preached around the world.

But being a missionary at heart, Sundar longed to take the gospel into the mysterious and forbidden land of Tibet. In April 1929, spurning the advice of friends, he set out into the Himalayan foothills, heading upward and inward, disappearing from sight. *He was never seen again.*

"It is a joy," he once said, "to suffer for my Savior. In bearing my cross, I hope to direct men to His cross. It was that cross that lifted me out of despair into the peace of God, and in the cross of Christ alone I will ever glory."

Meeting the Savior

My dad, Colonel David H. Arp Sr., was not a Christian and would not talk about spiritual issues. He passed away recently but not before praying to receive Christ—literally on his deathbed.

Dad took pride in his career as an army officer. He earned the Legion of Merit with two oak-leaf clusters, the Bronze Star, the French Croix de Guerre, and many other medals and citations. He was an aid to General George Patton during World War II and later to General Mark Clark during the occupation in Vienna, Austria.

For several years, Dad had been in failing health due to a form of Parkinson's disease called super nuclear palsy. He lost the ability to walk and to feed himself, and my aunt and a live-in nurse took care of him.

On Friday, April 30, 1999, I received a call. Dad was in intensive care and was not expected to live through the night. I caught the next flight to be with him, and my sister flew in from Denver. On Saturday, Dad seemed to rally. Then on Sunday morning, my sister told me that the nurse heard him call out during the night; he had very audibly, and repeatedly, cried, "Holy Jesus, pray for me."

We went into his room, and I asked him if he had called out for Jesus. He was not able to speak, but we used eye blinks to get yes or no answers. Two blinks were a yes—He blinked twice! I then asked him if he wanted to invite Jesus into his life to forgive his sins, and he blinked twice again! I told him that if it was the true desire of his heart to receive Christ, then he should pray silently with me. Afterwards I told him that Jesus was waiting for him in heaven and that Mom, his mother and dad, and other friends were waiting for him too. In fact, I remarked, "Mom is probably scurrying around to find the right outfit to wear when you arrive." Dad broke out in a BIG smile—the only time he smiled through the whole ordeal.

That morning, Dad was in a lot of pain. Though he had been given some morphine, we asked the nurse if the dose could be increased. She said it couldn't without a doctor's permission, and on Sunday morning, doctors were scarce. We prayed to find a doctor, and just then a white coat flashed by the door—Dad's doctor! Dad received a higher dose of morphine and soon fell into a deep sleep.

Five mornings later, he peacefully went to be with the Lord. On Monday, May 10, he was buried next to Mom in their hometown. His funeral included full military honors, complete with a twenty-one-gun salute.

Dad finally saw Jesus.

David Arp

THE LOST SHEEP

Diana Ellington was too tired to pray and too worried to sleep. Her daughter was in deep trouble.

There had been problems with Michelle since childhood, but the concerns became crises during the teen years as she started smoking, drugging, skipping school, and dressing in black. A friend lured her into Satanism, and she began living in a house with two warlocks and three witches. She soon learned how to channel spirits, cast spells, and ply the darkest waters of the supernatural.

With a mother's breaking heart, Diana groaned as she heard of Michelle—egged on by friends and fiends—biting people, drawing their blood, and drinking it.

Frantic and desperate, she confronted her daughter as often as she dared, but futilely. On one occasion, Diana narrowly escaped harm as a possessed Michelle lunged at her, trying to slit her throat with a knife. It was the family dog who intervened, charging at Michelle and biting her wrist, and saved Diana from injury.

Finally Diana realized there was nothing left to do but to ask her friends to

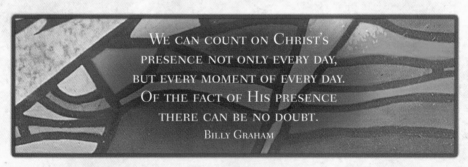

WE CAN COUNT ON CHRIST'S PRESENCE NOT ONLY EVERY DAY, BUT EVERY MOMENT OF EVERY DAY. OF THE FACT OF HIS PRESENCE THERE CAN BE NO DOUBT.
BILLY GRAHAM

join her in earnest, effectual prayer—
that's when things began to change.
Michelle was pregnant when her
boyfriend left her, and as her other
support systems began falling away,
she became lonely and thoughtful.

Diana prayed harder.

Michelle eventually sank into
depression and began feeling terribly
frightened. She felt as though
magnetic forces were drawing her,
despite her protests, toward God.

Diana remained earnest in prayer.

Michelle, feeling guilty and dirty,
began to grow tired of the life she was
living.

Diana pressed her friends to keep
praying.

Appropriately, it was during the
Halloween season that Michelle fell to
her knees and begged God to take
away her pain. She gave up the sins of

her past, renounced the enemy, and
turned in simple faith to Jesus Christ.

"Mom," Diana said, after coming
home at last, "I just never had a chance
against your prayers."

Freedom in Christ

I was always a shy, quiet girl. My mother called me homely; my stepdad called me ugly. One night at dinner, when I was about eleven, my stepdad slammed his silverware down on the table and angrily said that he could no longer stand to look at my face while he ate. We never ate together as a family again.

One day I came home from school to find that my stepdad had given my favorite dolls and a blue ink pen to my two-year-old half sister. The ink on my dolls never washed off—and neither did my hurt feelings. As I got older, Mother would accuse me of doing things that I never did. Fights became frequent. She said I was a failure

"I will never leave you nor forsake you."
Hebrews 13:5

and would never amount to anything. I remember wanting someone to love me, hug me, and tell me I was okay.

I began dreaming of running away early in my sophomore year of high school. I rebelled and looked for ways to escape. A wise counselor encouraged me to endure until I graduated. I did, but graduation did not bring the freedom I sought. Mother had decided that I could not leave home until I was of legal age, which was four months away! When I could stand it no longer, I ran away. But I knew it was wrong, and I came back home. Then I was locked in my room.

When I was caught trying to run away

28

again, I was sent to a youth home. A month later, my mother legally disowned me, and I was released to a foster family. Two months later, I turned eighteen and was set free.

But I really wasn't free. I was held captive by the anger and hatred I felt toward my mother and stepfather. This anger attacked every relationship I tried to have. I looked for freedom in relationships, alcohol, drugs, religion, and women's lib, but freedom eluded me. I was in bondage to the cruel words I had heard as a child. Fear, rejection, and self-pity kept me imprisoned. Fits of jealousy, outbursts of anger, depression, and uncontrollable crying ruled my life. I hated myself, and much of the time, I longed to die!

In 1980, I was invited by a friend to attend a neighborhood Bible study. While there, I was introduced to the One whose love would open the prison doors of my heart and truly set me free. That day, He gave me a new life! By His grace, my anger and hatred gave way to love, compassion, forgiveness, and understanding.

I still suffer from the scars of my past, but I am no longer imprisoned by them. Jesus died to set the captives free . . . from sin . . . and from death.

Yes! He loves me . . . the Bible tells me so!

Karla

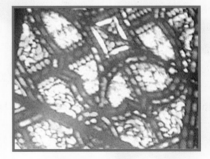

A Gentle Surprise

In February 1997, I was on retreat with about sixty teenagers. We broke into small prayer groups and began to share some of the troubles in each of our lives.

As we went around our small circle, each teenager shared a story. Sometimes it was about a very serious problem, such as drugs, unwanted pregnancy, trouble with the law, or the inability to communicate with parents. I sat and listened to their trials, and silently, I lifted each one up in prayer. At the end of the sharing time, they looked at me and asked me to share about the heaviest crosses I felt at this point in my life.

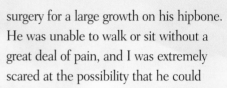

I told them that on Friday, my youngest son was scheduled to have surgery for a large growth on his hipbone. He was unable to walk or sit without a great deal of pain, and I was extremely scared at the possibility that he could have cancer. I also shared with them that my oldest son and I had become estranged during Christmas because of religious differences and that I was not permitted to see my grandchildren.

At that moment, the young adults in my group prayed for me, and I began to cry. Moved with compassion and love, they hugged me, and at that moment I felt a deep sense of the presence of God. It was the most moving experience I've felt in all the years that I have taught religious education.

Chris Luley

Out of Control

I was twenty-eight years old, living in a house on the beach, driving a Porsche, wearing custom-made suits, making lots of money, and dating a beautiful woman. Life was great!

But I wasn't happy. When I looked in the mirror, I didn't like what I saw. On the outside, I was successful, but I felt insignificant. Inside, I was embarrassed and afraid, and I felt like a failure. I appeared to have everything going for me. But I was out of control.

A few years earlier, I had tasted the sweet victory of success. Then my priorities got messed up. I never intended for it to become a habit, but two years later, I was addicted to cocaine. It was costing me a thousand dollars a week. My girlfriend Sheryl and I would get high four days out of seven. My addiction got so bad that even my dealer told me to slow down.

I lost my edge in all areas. I was reckless, made poor decisions, lost my job, gained forty pounds, went through my savings, sold stocks and bonds to pay for my addiction, and spiritually felt dead!

One evening, I went for a jog while several grams of cocaine were racing through my body. When I returned home, my heart was beating in a way that made me feel as if I was going to die. But the feeling subsided . . . and I lived. The next

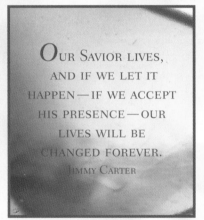

OUR SAVIOR LIVES, AND IF WE LET IT HAPPEN — IF WE ACCEPT HIS PRESENCE — OUR LIVES WILL BE CHANGED FOREVER.
JIMMY CARTER

morning, the newspaper ran a story about a famous basketball star who had died from cocaine intoxication. That was a wake-up call for me!

I had been drifting for years as a Christian, and I knew I was powerless and broken. I needed to quit the insanity! I needed to save my life, but I couldn't! I had tried over one hundred times to quit my cocaine and alcohol addictions, but I had always failed. I also knew that Jesus had power—and I needed that power!

Falling on my knees, I prayed for the power of the Holy Spirit to help me conquer this destructive behavior. I wanted to glorify God but could not do it on my own. I found my escape and the answers I was looking for through prayer and studying the Bible daily.

I started living a different life. I learned that if I stayed close to Him, He would get me through the times when I was tempted. Since that day, over thirteen years ago, I have not touched cocaine.

He saved my life on this earth, and I know my future is secured forever!

Todd Duncan

Praise You

We decided to travel to Puerto Rico to combine vacation with some work time . . .

One day while the children played at the water's edge with my mother (who was always the biggest "kid" of all), Bill and I took a walk down the beach. . . . We were still quite a distance away when we saw a child running toward us, waving his arms. As we got closer we could tell it was Benjy, and he was urgently trying to tell us something. We ran to meet him.

"Suzanne lost her glasses in the ocean!" he was yelling over the thunder of the surf. "She was picking up shells and a big wave came in and knocked off her glasses. The tide washed them out to sea!"

"How long ago?" I asked, thinking about how quickly the strong currents here had been carrying things—and children—down the beach before we could even notice.

"About fifteen minutes ago. We've been

looking for them ever since." . . .

By now we were shouting back and forth to Suzanne. "Where did you lose them?" I asked.

"Right here. I was standing right here!"

She was knee-deep in water, as the tide was coming in. "I can't see a thing, mother. What are we going to do?"

"Let's pray," I said, and I took her two hands in mine.

Then I thought to myself, "What are you doing? You're going to ruin this child's faith. Those glasses have been long since pulled out to sea by the undertow and have most likely been smashed to bits against the coral reef. If we even find any pieces they will have washed ashore far down the beach!" But I was too far into this to turn back now. Holding Suzanne's hands and standing knee-deep in water, I prayed: "Jesus, you

know how much Suzanne needs her glasses, and that we are far from home and know no doctors to have them replaced here. We are your children and this is your ocean. You know where the glasses are so we're asking You to send them back . . ."

Just then Suzanne squeezed my hand and interrupted my prayer. "Mother! Something just hit my leg!" She let go of my hand, reached down into the water, and pulled out her glasses. They were in one piece and not even scratched.

We danced a jig of praise, and she ran off to tell the others who were searching the beach farther down.

Much later that evening, after we'd had our dinner and the kids were ready for bed, I took out the Bible and opened it to the Psalms to read something that might fit the sounds of the surf pounding the shore outside our room's open patio doors. I chose a psalm we'd read many times but never had we heard it like we did that night.

. . . This is too glorious, too wonderful to believe. I can never be lost to your spirit! I can never get away from my God! If I go up to heaven, you are there; if I go down to the place of the dead, you are there. If I ride the morning winds to the farthest oceans, even there your hand will guide me, your strength will support me . . .

When we had finished all of Psalm 139, we could hardly believe that God's Word had been so specific for us . . . so familiar in this faraway island, yet as new and fresh as this day's miracle. . . .

Psalm 139 has interfaced with our family many times since then. Our children are now reading it to their children. Soon after that trip Bill and I wrote that psalm into a song we called "Praise You." It has been arranged for choirs and recorded by various artists. But it will always be for us a reminder of the day a little girl prayed with her mother on an island beach for a pair of glasses lost at sea.

Gloria Gaither

SISTERLY LOVE

Edith Morgan of Roan Mountain, Tennessee, was in the third grade when the Great Depression swept over Appalachia, forcing her brother Donnie, who was seventeen, to leave the mountains for work in Ohio. The checks he sent home every week allowed the family to survive. But it was a cruel separation. Edith dearly loved her big brother, and a long year passed before he was given a week's vacation.

One day as class ended, one of the girls told me she had seen my brother Donnie walking up the road. I got so excited that I rushed out the door and started running the two miles home. I was out of breath when I ran through the door and found Donnie.

She flew into his arms with such hysterical crying that to console her, Donnie reached into his pocket and gave her his fountain pen. She had never had a fountain pen before. It was the kind that when turned upside down and unscrewed could be refilled from a bottle of ink. That pen became her pride and joy.

One day I couldn't find my pen. I searched every inch of the house, every room, every closet. We had been taught to take our problems to the Lord, so I slipped out behind the pile of lumber in the orchard, got down on my knees, and prayed desperately that God would help me find my pen. But I had prayed many times for other things and was a little doubtful. So I said, "Now, Father, answer this prayer. If you won't do anything else, I ask you to do this."

No sooner had I spoken these words than I felt guilty about them. I got back on my knees and asked God to forgive me for speaking so brashly. Then I asked Him again to help me find my pen.

Getting up, I went immediately to the house, marched to the back bedroom, raised the lid of the old trunk that was full of rags and strings from mother's quilts, and plunged my hand into the scraps. There among the strings and scraps I felt my pen. I suspect my mother threw it in there because it made such a mess when I tried to refill it. But regardless, God had answered my prayer.

"And that," Edith Morgan says today, "is how I first learned that Jesus hears our prayers and answers our sincere requests."

All for the Lord

All I ever wanted to do in life was play the drums and make music for God. I knew He gave me my talent, and music was my lifeline to Him. I played drums professionally for twenty years and was in a Christian band. I also taught music and was a drum instructor for professional parades.

But today, I can no longer hold the drumsticks. For years, I thought I would get better, but now I know that I will not get better.

Though I've had strange symptoms of weakness since childhood, it wasn't until I was twenty-nine that I was finally diagnosed with a rare disease that attacks the outercoating of the nerves called syringomyelia. It affects all parts of the body, including the organs and the respiratory system. Only about one hundred people have been diagnosed with this disease in the United States.

At the time of diagnosis, my doctor seemed to have a defeatist attitude. He told me to go home, get in bed, and wait to die. After receiving this shocking news, I felt sorry for myself for about a year. I even went into a hospice program two different times, but I was a real challenge to them. Though the organization is wonderful, I could not get my time schedule connected with theirs—I felt there were still other things God wanted me to do. I finally realized that *the doctor is not God!*

Even though I could no longer play the drums, which I loved doing, I could still teach, write music, and sing. I thought that all was lost when the ability to play the drums was taken away from me, but I now understand that I am just a vehicle to be used in whatever way is pleasing to Him. I feel that because *He wants to use all of me* and not just my hands, He changed the desires of my heart. *And I will never be the same again.*

It has been six years since my diagnosis, and I am still alive with things to be thankful for. I am living with a couple from my church, Vickie (another Christian singer) and her husband Greg. They have taken me into their family and, out of love, help me get through my day-to-day living.

Vickie and I are working on a music project and plan to have it ready at the beginning of 2000. I realize that I might not live to see our music project completed—or this book project completed—but I have seen Him bring me this far. The legacy I leave will be my words and my music, which I hope will encourage others.

My pastor has helped me plan my funeral and my memorial service. I know I am dying, but I also know where I am going. These words from one of our songs bring me great comfort as I wait: "I am safe . . . Though I may not understand . . . I am where I should be . . . in the Father's hands."

Kim Hyden

The Holy Comforter

A wonderful friend of mine, Agnes Frazier, told me that for fifty years, she and her husband Emit shared a Bible reading and prayer at the breakfast table. When Emit died, Agnes went to bed thinking that she could never again start the day with devotional exercises.

But the next morning, she bravely sat at the kitchen table and opened her Bible to the spot where she and her husband had quit their reading only twenty-four hours before. As she began to read Isaiah 54, the verse that stared up at her was the fifth one: *For your Maker is your husband, the Lord of hosts is His name . . .*

She smiled and said,
"Thank you, Lord."

Pastor Rob Morgan

We knew He was dead
"It is finished!" He said
We had watched as His life ebbed away
Then we all stood around
'Til the guards took Him down
Joseph begged for His body that day

It was late afternoon
When we got to the tomb
Wrapped His body and sealed up the grave
So I know how you feel
His death was so real
But please listen and hear what I say

I've just seen Jesus

I tell you He's alive

I've just seen Jesus

Our precious Lord alive

And I knew, He really saw me too

As if 'til now I'd never lived

All that I'd done before

Won't matter anymore

I've just seen Jesus

And I'll never be the same again

Depression Does That to a Person

You can't always tell what is going on inside people by the way they look on the outside. I usually look normal. I have been married eighteen years but only about one or two of those years has been "normal," at least as the world knows normalcy.

Before the proper mental illness diagnosis was made, I was told I had demons inside of me. I was thankful for the correct diagnosis of manic depression and multiple personality disorder.

I was hospitalized for many years, and even now, I go to the hospital when a crisis occurs. People wonder how I can be a Christian and still have these conditions, which can also lead to self-harm. But I know that *depression does that to a person.* It helps me to think about people of great faith who also faced depression, such as Jeremiah, David, and Elijah.

Years ago, people with my conditions would have been put away or kept hidden. But there is freedom in being able to trust someone enough to talk about my depression and reach out to others. On good days, you will find me chatty, loving, caring, able to pray, and giving to others. At times, reading the Bible can pull me through dark memories from my past.

On a bad day, I am thankful for those who, in love, reach out to me. During tough times, you will find me unwilling to look in the mirror, terrified, crying, not eating, hearing voices that are not there, and longing for the darkness or the blessing of death. *Depression does that to a person.*

Sometimes, I get lost and can't find

Whereas I was blind, I — now I see.

my way home. Sometimes, I am afraid to go out of the front door or into the backyard. Sometimes, I sob for hours for no logical reason. Sometimes, the stimulus of the world is so overwhelming that I can't cope and I retreat into the "safety" of another personality or into the comfort of darkness. *Depression does that to a person.*

For me to function on a daily basis, I need the help of my husband, my Christian therapist, my psychiatrist, my close friends, my medication, *and* my Jesus. This is my life.

But, even on my darkest days, I can still say *I've seen Jesus* . . . with my spiritual eyes. I can feel His presence. I'm thankful He is my savior, for without Him . . . I know I would be dead.

Sharon Paul

A PASSION FOR CHRIST

The mud walls of his small Ethiopian hovel are lined with newspapers, and his primitive furniture is formed from cowhides stretched over wooden frames. Food is scarce for his wife and five children, and life is hard.

But life is sweet, too. "I have a lot of needs," Negussie Tameru says, "but I have peace in Christ."

It wasn't always so. Negussie Tameru resorted to banditry as a teenager, learning early to ambush, rob, and kill. He also became enmeshed in sorcery and idolatry. At age eighteen, he was charged with murder and sentenced to prison. Upon his release, however, he plunged immediately into his old ways. The police intervened again, taking away his gun,

> *I*N ORDER TO HOPE
> FOR SALVATION
> FROM GOD, MAN
> MUST STOP
> BENEATH CHRIST'S
> CROSS.
> POPE JOHN PAUL II

warning him so sternly that Negussie actually applied for a legitimate job. Against the advice of locals, he was hired by a Baptist mission as security guard.

There he was intrigued by the Bible and actually saved two days' wages to purchase his own copy. He had little education, and this was the first book Negussie had ever attempted to read. As he thumbed it open, his eyes fell on Revelation 21:7–8, "He who overcomes shall inherit all things, and I will be his God and he shall be My son. But the cowardly, unbelieving, abominable, murderers, sexually immoral, sorcerers, idolaters, and all liars shall have their part in the lake which burns with fire and brimstone, which is the second death."

The words *murderer . . . sorcerer . . .*

idolater . . . burned a hole in his brain, and, terrified, he quickly put his Bible away. "I got real scared and decided this was a bad book," he recalls, "so I hid it."

But shortly afterward, an Ethiopian believer at the mission compound approached Negussie, offering to tell him some "good news." It was the good news of forgiveness through Jesus Christ, and Negussie devoured the message like a starving man. "I cried and cried and cried that day," he says. "I couldn't believe God would forgive me—not for all the things I'd done." He immediately took the message to his wife and children. To his joy, every one of them converted.

The message of Christ radiated from their home. Now he pastors a small church in Shola Gebeya, Ethiopia, spending his days sharing the gospel with neighboring villages and peoples.

His passion for Christ is evident.

"What really scares me," he once said, "is that on the Judgment Day, we'll all be standing around the throne, and my neighbors will point at me and ask, 'Why didn't you tell me?'

M. P. PAINE

When I was growing up in Victoria, British Columbia, my parents couldn't afford shoes and books. So I quit school at age eleven and went to work delivering groceries. I gave the money I earned to my mother, who gave me back twenty-five cents. I loved to read and spent most of my money buying books . . .

My parents used to take me to church by horse and buggy every Sunday, but after I married in 1930, I stopped going. I came to believe that there was no God, that religion was all a superstition.

Yet I knew that there was more to life than what I had. I was searching for the meaning of my existence. I turned to writers and philosophers hoping to find a purpose for living but was always disappointed.

I eventually became a successful and wealthy businessman. In my sixties, however, a series of tragedies struck.

I suffered a stroke, from which I spent two years recovering. Then I lost all my money in an unfortunate business deal.

On October 30, 1976, when I was sixty-eight years old, I sat in my room contemplating suicide. I was in pain from

arthritis, a bad back, and weakness. But more, I was hurting in my mind . . . I had nowhere to turn; I was desperate and hopeless.

Then I remembered a message given by Billy Graham at the close of one of his Crusades. I had seen it on TV while waiting for the next program. Mr. Graham had encouraged the audience to surrender their lives to Jesus Christ.

Now I thought, "What if he's right

about God?" Then I leaned forward in my chair and tried to repeat the prayer that Mr. Graham had prayed. "Lord, I am a sinner. I am sorry," I said. Then I added, "Jesus, if You are there, show Yourself."

When I leaned back in my chair, I knew Christ. My entire body was filled with warmth, the aching stopped, and I was at peace. After so many years of searching for the truth in books, I finally found Truth in the Person of Jesus Christ. The next day I bought a Bible and soon joined an evangelical church.

At the age of seventy-five I felt called to the small town of Stewart in northern British Columbia. Carrying my Bible, I knocked on three hundred doors. I found two Christians, and we held three revival meetings with the help of an Indian pastor. Afterward, an evangelical church was founded in that area.

Decision magazine

To Have This Moment

Several years back my wife, Gloria, and I found some time in our schedules to take a January vacation at a secluded spot on Florida's west coast. We were away from the recording studio, the  office, the concert stage, the TV studio, every professional distraction except the telephone. I couldn't imagine being away from that modern lifeline.

On our way to dinner the first evening, Gloria exclaimed over the beautiful sunset she'd seen. Pink clouds, swaying palms, reflecting sea. "Tomorrow night, I promise, we'll enjoy it together," I said.

But the next evening, just as the sun was dipping into the sea, I answered the phone, and it was someone I had to talk to. "Come on," Gloria beckoned. With my hand over the receiver, I protested,

"I have to take this."

"Hurry up," she said.

By the time I joined her on the beach, the sun was a rind of orange on the horizon—just enough light to see her angry shrug. Suffice it to say, the evening was ruined. Throughout dinner I argued how important it was to talk to hard-to-reach people when you had the chance, and how we couldn't do all our singing, speaking, and writing if we weren't disciplined. Gloria maintained that some things just had to wait. Weren't we in Florida to enjoy each other's company without interruptions?

She was right, of course. I usually end up scurrying around to get things done while she knows better how to be still and savor the moment. I should know better. We've written a song "We Have This Moment Today," with lyrics that say: "Yesterday's gone, and tomorrow may never come / But we have this moment today." I promised Gloria I would do better. Three years later we were on a plane—just the two of us, on our way to another much-needed vacation. In mid flight I took out the manuscript of my latest book. Pencil in hand, I went over it for the hundredth time. I caught myself when I came to the anecdote about the missed sunset in Florida.

I leaned my head back and closed my eyes. Dear Lord, I prayed, thanks for the reminder. I put the manuscript away and covered Gloria's hand with mine.

Work, as much as I am grateful to God for it, could wait. My office would do just fine without me. The world didn't need me to be on the phone to keep it going. Nothing, I vowed, was going to make me miss another sunset with my wife.

Bill Gaither

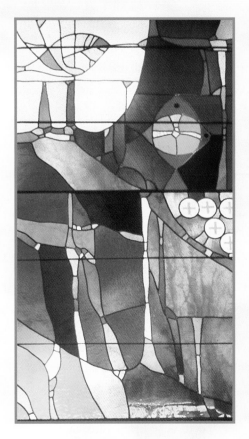

DIVINE FORGIVENESS

"*You* pastors and priests!" the woman snapped. "You are a bunch of thieves and liars and crooks. All you want is money!"

It was November 1965, and in the studios of Radio HCJB in Quito, Ecuador, Maria Benitez-Perez, a Communist leader, was chewing out the renowned evangelist Luis Palau. She bellowed for more than twenty minutes, swearing and smoking all the while. But at length, her vitriol waned, and she wearily began telling Palau the sad story of her life. She finally ended with these words: "Hey, Palau, supposing there is a God—which there isn't—but just supposing there is, do you think He would take a woman like me?"

Palau, having listened patiently, now turned to Hebrews 10:17 and quoted these words: "Their sins and their lawless deeds I will remember no more."

"I don't believe in the Bible," she countered.

"But we're just supposing there's a God, right? Let's suppose this is His Word. He says, 'Their sins and their lawless deeds I will remember no more.'"

"But listen, I've been an adulteress, married three times, and in bed with a lot of men."

"Their sins and their lawless deeds I will remember no more."

Seventeen times Maria flung out objections, and seventeen times Louis Palau quietly quoted Hebrews 10:17.

Finally, her arguments and anger spent, Maria bowed her head and offered a simple prayer, confessing her sins and asking Christ to be her Savior.

The next time Palau saw her, Maria's teeth were broken, and her face was marred by blotches and bruises, the result of an attack that occurred after she announced her conversion at a Communist meeting. Amid danger and death threats, Maria went into hiding, but the Marxists were eager to track her down, fearful she would betray their secretly planned revolution in June.

When agents eventually found her, she somehow persuaded them to retreat to her father's farm where she gave them Christian books to read. Then, on the morning of the planned revolution, the Communist party leader came to see her.

"Maria," he asked, "Why did you become a Christian?"

As she shared her testimony, he listened carefully. And when she handed him a Bible and a copy of Billy Graham's book *Peace With God,* he began reading them on the spot.

Later that day, the planned June 1966 overthrow of Ecuador's government failed to materialize—The revolutionary leaders were at Maria's father's farm, reading about Jesus.

GATHERING THE HARVEST

On October 8, 1934, a harried southern evangelist sat alone in his hotel room, dejected and discouraged. His campaign was faltering, the newspapers were blasting him, the churches were fighting him, and he seemed powerless to do go any good. Sighing deeply, he took a sheet of hotel stationary and wrote out this prayer:

Dear Father: Thou knowest the conduct of all in this town: how the Antichrist has made his power felt; how the ministers have opposed.

Father, please, for Thy Name's sake and Thy Son's sake, begin to deal with these: the scoffers and the enemies. Deal with the Baptists, my own Brotherhood . . . the Methodists and their leaders . . . [with all those against You in any denomination . . .]

Deal with the newspapers. O Lord, You know how the testimony of Jesus has been opposed in this city. Deal with the city councilmen and all that would try to drive us out of the city . . .

O Dear Lord, come on Thy servant and make his messages a burning fire. Lord, give us a Pentecost here . . . O Lord, please come to the help of Thy servant. Dear Father, make this the greatest meeting we have ever witnessed. Pour out Thy Spirit tomorrow. Dear Lord, may this city be made to tremble . . .

O Lord, I need Your endorsement, and show this city that You are with me.

In His Name . . .

The evangelist signed his name at the end of his prayer—*M. F. Ham.*

As He often does, the Lord answered his prayer beyond all expectation. For among Mordecai Ham's converts during that 1934 campaign in Charlotte, North Carolina, was Frank Graham's tall, blue-eyed son *Billy.*

THE POWER OF GOD'S WORD

In 1934, Adolf Hitler summoned German church leaders to his Berlin office. There, he berated them for insufficiently supporting his programs. Pastor Martin Niemoller explained that he was concerned only for the welfare of the church and of the German people.

Hitler snapped, "You confine yourself to the church. I'll take care of the German people." Niemoller replied, "We too, as Christians and churchmen, have a responsibility toward the German people. That responsibility was entrusted to us by God, and neither you nor anyone in this world has the power to take it from us."

> JESUS SAID TO HER, "I AM THE RESURRECTION AND THE LIFE. HE WHO BELIEVES IN ME, THOUGH HE MAY DIE, HE SHALL LIVE."
> JOHN 11:25

Hitler listened in silence, but that evening the Gestapo raided Niemoller's rectory. A few days later, a bomb exploded in Niemoller's church. During the months following, he was closely watched by the secret police until he was eventually arrested and placed in solitary confinement.

Dr. Niemoller's trial began on February 7, 1938. That morning, a green-uniformed guard escorted the minister from his prison cell, through a series of underground passages toward the courtroom. Niemoller was overcome with dread and loneliness. What would become of him? Of his family? His church? What terrors and tortures awaited them all?

The guard's face was impassive, and he was silent as stone. But as they exited a tunnel to ascend a final flight of stairs, Niemoller heard a whisper. At first he didn't know where it came from, for the voice was as soft as a sigh. Then he realized the officer was breathing into his ear the words of Proverbs 18:10: *The name of the Lord is a strong tower; the righteous run to it and are safe.*

Niemoller's fear fell away, courage rose in his heart, and the power of that verse sustained him through his trial—and his ensuing years in Nazi concentration camps.

THE GREAT PHYSICIAN

Frank Kuntz got his first taste of homelessness at age five, when his mother deserted him and his father had a heart attack. During ensuing years, Frank was tossed from family to family and was physically and sexually abused. Badly troubled at the age of sixteen, he assaulted a man with a tire iron. Only by joining the marines did he avoid prison, but he started drinking and using drugs. For him, Vietnam was an endless medicine chest of illegal drugs.

One night during his second tour of duty in Vietnam, he led his men on a patrol. There in the jungles, in the darkness, and stifling heat, he saw flashes of light from enemy positions, and Frank felt himself dropping to a prone position. When he opened his eyes six days later, he was in a hospital in Okinawa; his left side was blown away, his leg badly damaged, his hip shattered. The doctor started to amputate, but Frank's marine buddy's father, an orthopedic surgeon in California, flew immediately to Japan and saved his leg.

Once out of the service, Frank did well for himself. He married, started several businesses, and in time surpassed even the American dream—a beautiful wife, three children, millions of dollars in assets, nice vacations. But Frank was still drinking heavily, still using drugs—the hidden seams of his life were unraveling. In the divorce, his wife took the children and most of his possessions.

Frank's addictions increased, even as he started designing the tiled areas of expensive homes and buildings. When his work was featured in *Better Homes and Gardens*, he again seemed on the verge of success.

Then a call came, asking him to bid on the tiling for the new arena in Nashville, Tennessee. As he toured the unfinished building, a workman bumped into him, sending him plunging down three flights of seats. The fall ripped open his old war wounds. Later that same night, his truck and equipment were stolen.

This time Frank couldn't pull himself from the brink. Within a month, he found himself limping on crutches, panhandling for money, living under bridges—homeless, hateful, and hurting.

His hunger drove him to the Nashville Union Mission, but once there, he didn't want to leave. "Three squares a day," he recalls. "A bed at night. Clean sheets. Showers. People to help me around.

What more could I have wanted?"

One night while attending an evangelical service in the mission's chapel, he seemed to hear the Gospel for the first time. The preacher was speaking from Philippians 1:6: *"He who has begun a good work in you will complete it until the day of Jesus Christ."*

Needing God's workmanship in his shattered life, Frank bowed at the altar and gave his heart to the Christ.

The change was instant and astounding. "The Lord moved in, and it was as if He put all my depression and hatred into a bottle and threw it away," he recalls.

Today Frank Kuntz is director of operations for transient ministries at Nashville Union Mission, helping down-and-outers like himself find the Great Physician of the soul who has done so much for him.

FROM THE PUBLISHER

The words *I've Just Seen Jesus* bring instant attention to the hearer and present a wonderful mental picture that is the heart's desire of most Christians.

We are thankful to all who revealed their hearts and their stories in this book with the hope of imparting encouragement and inspiration as well as the reassurance that our Lord is truly alive and comes to us in many different ways. These are lives that were touched for His glory.

Our prayer is for your heart and your spiritual eyes to see Jesus in such a way that you will be impressed to share your story with others, offering it as a blessing to those around you. Like many of you, Marsha, my wife, and I have our own stories in which the Lord made Himself evident in our lives . . . changing us, never to be the same again.

We are extremely grateful to our friends—Larnelle Harris, Sandi Patty, Danny Daniels, and Bill and Gloria Gaither—for bringing to us and to the world this wonderful, dynamic song in such a magnificent fashion.

Jack Countryman
Touching Lives . . . Changing Lives

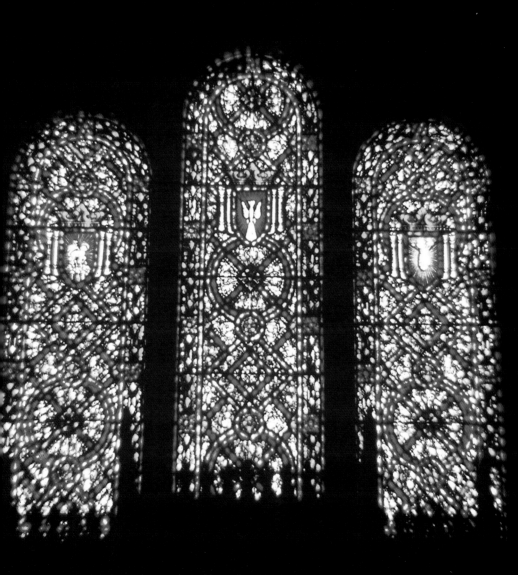

Acknowledgements

Special thanks are made to those who graciously shared their stories in this book. Material previously published is accredited to the following:

Divine Forgiveness. Taken from *World Vision* magazine, "Evangelism IS Social Action," by Luis Palau, April-May 1990. Reprinted by permission of World Vision, copyright © 1990.

M. P. Paine. Taken from *Decision* magazine, "M. P. Paine," by M. P. Paine, July-August 1991; copyright © Billy Graham Evangelistic Association, used by permission, all rights reserved.

A Passion for Christ. Source: International Mission Board.

The Power of God's Word. Adapted from *On This Day* by Robert Morgan. Copyright © 1997. Used by permission of Thomas Nelson Publishers.

Praise You. Taken from *Because He Lives* by Gloria Gaither. Copyright © 1997 by Gloria and William J. Gaither. Used by permission of Zondervan Publishing House.

To Have This Moment. Used by permission of Gloria Cassity Stargel.

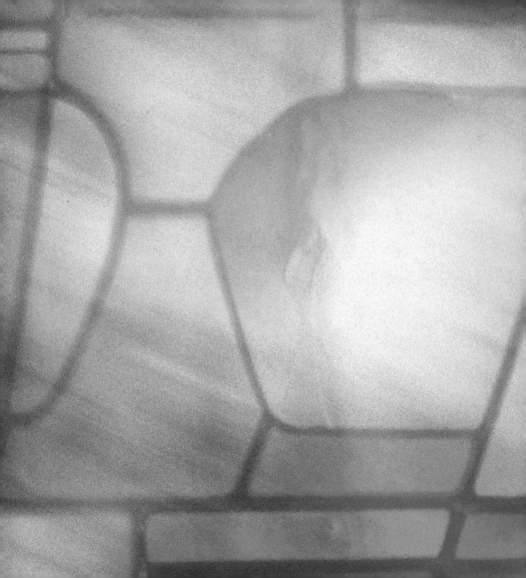